Greetings from
HARTFORD
CONN.

Greetings from
HARTFORD
CONN.

Greetings from
HARTFORD
CONN.

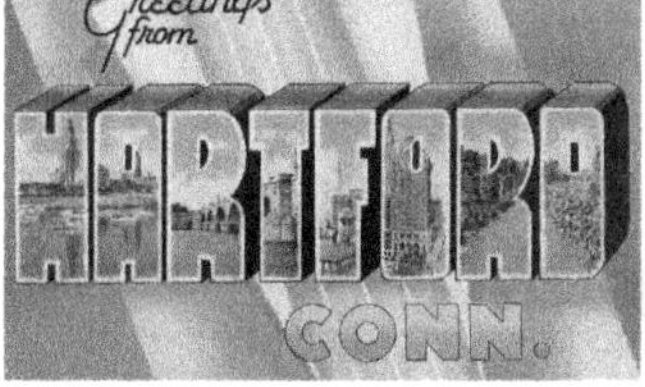
Greetings from
HARTFORD
CONN.

Greetings from
HARTFORD
CONN.

Greetings from
HARTFORD
CONN.

Greetings from
HARTFORD
CONN.

Greetings from
HARTFORD
CONN.

Greetings from
HARTFORD
CONN.

Greetings from
HARTFORD
CONN.

Greetings from
HARTFORD
CONN.

Greetings from
HARTFORD
CONN.

Greetings from
HARTFORD
CONN.

Greetings from
HARTFORD
CONN.

Greetings from
HARTFORD
CONN.

Greetings from
HARTFORD
CONN.

Greetings from
HARTFORD
CONN.

Greetings from
HARTFORD
CONN.

Greetings from
HARTFORD
CONN.

Greetings from
HARTFORD
CONN.

Greetings from
HARTFORD
CONN.

Greetings from
HARTFORD
CONN.

Greetings from
HARTFORD
CONN.

Greetings from
HARTFORD
CONN.

Greetings from
HARTFORD
CONN.

Greetings from
HARTFORD
CONN.

Greetings from
HARTFORD
CONN.

Greetings from
HARTFORD
CONN.

Greetings from
HARTFORD
CONN.

Greetings from
HARTFORD
CONN.

Greetings from
HARTFORD
CONN.

Greetings from
HARTFORD
CONN.

Greetings from
HARTFORD
CONN.

Greetings from
HARTFORD
CONN.

Greetings from
HARTFORD
CONN.

Greetings from
HARTFORD
CONN.

Greetings from
HARTFORD
CONN.

Greetings from
HARTFORD
CONN.

Greetings from
HARTFORD
CONN.

Greetings from
HARTFORD
CONN.

Greetings from
HARTFORD
CONN.

Greetings from
HARTFORD
CONN.

Greetings from
HARTFORD
CONN.

Greetings from
HARTFORD
CONN.

Greetings from
HARTFORD
CONN.

Greetings from
HARTFORD
CONN.

Greetings from
HARTFORD
CONN.

Greetings from
HARTFORD
CONN.

Greetings from
HARTFORD
CONN.

Greetings from
HARTFORD
CONN.

Greetings from
HARTFORD
CONN.

Greetings from
HARTFORD
CONN.

Greetings from
HARTFORD
CONN.

Greetings from
HARTFORD
CONN.

Greetings from
HARTFORD
CONN.

Greetings from
HARTFORD
CONN.

Greetings from
HARTFORD
CONN.

Greetings from
HARTFORD
CONN.

Greetings from
HARTFORD
CONN.

Greetings from
HARTFORD
CONN.

Greetings from
HARTFORD
CONN.

Greetings from
HARTFORD
CONN.

Greetings from
HARTFORD
CONN.

Greetings from
HARTFORD
CONN.

Greetings from
HARTFORD
CONN.

Greetings from
HARTFORD
CONN.

Greetings from
HARTFORD
CONN.

Greetings from
HARTFORD
CONN.

Greetings from
HARTFORD
CONN.

Greetings from
HARTFORD
CONN.

Greetings from
HARTFORD
CONN.

Greetings from
HARTFORD
CONN.

Greetings from
HARTFORD
CONN.

Greetings from
HARTFORD
CONN.

Greetings from
HARTFORD
CONN.

Printed in the USA
CPSIA information can be obtained
at www.ICGtesting.com
LVHW041211080624
782687LV00002B/169

9 798385 406371